DEMOCRACY— AMERICAN STYLE

DEMOCRACY— AMERICAN STYLE

One Man's View on How to Make a Great Country Even Better

Herman M. Witten, Sr.

To order additional copies of this book, contact:
Xlibris Corporation
1-888-795-4274
www.Xlibris.com
Orders@Xlibris.com
41131

TABLE OF CONTENTS

This book is dedicated to

Melvin, Tracey and Sidney.

FOREWORD

This book is designed to do two things. They are:

1. To inform and/or remind the readers of America's ugly historical past when it comes to race.
2. To assist everyone who needs help before seriously beginning to talk about America's racial problems in hopes of reaching viable solutions.

When you see words that are in double quotes, it simply means that I question their validity. For example, the word "White," when referring to a group of people, does not reflect the truth.

Author

IN CONGRESS, July 4, 1776

The Declaration of Independence

When in the Course of human events, it becomes necessary for one people to dissolve the political bands which have connected them with another, and to assume among the powers of the earth, the separate and equal station to which the Laws of Nature and of Nature's God entitle them, a decent respect to the opinions of mankind requires that they should declare the causes which impel them to the separation.

We hold these truths to be self-evident, that all men are created equal, that they are endowed by their Creator with certain unalienable Rights, that among these are Life, Liberty and the pursuit of Happiness. That to secure these rights, Governments are instituted among Men, deriving their just powers from the consent of the governed, That whenever any Form of Government becomes destructive of these ends, it is the Right of the People to alter or to abolish it, and to institute new Government, laying its foundation on such principles and organizing its powers in such form, as to them shall seem most likely to effect their Safety and Happiness. Prudence, indeed, will dictate that Governments long established should not be changed for light and transient causes; and accordingly all experience hath shewn, that mankind are more disposed to suffer, while evils are sufferable, than to right themselves by abolishing the forms to which they are accustomed. But when a long train of abuses and usurpations, pursuing invariably the same Object evinces a design to reduce them under absolute Despotism, it is their right, it is their duty, to throw off such Government, and to provide new Guards for their future security. Such has been the patient sufferance of these Colonies; and such is now the necessity which constrains them to alter their former Systems of Government. The history of the present King of Great Britain is a history of repeated injuries and usurpations, all having in direct object the establishment of an absolute Tyranny over these States. To prove this, let Facts be submitted to a candid world.

He has refused his Assent to Laws, the most wholesome and necessary for the public good.

He has forbidden his Governors to pass Laws of immediate and pressing importance, unless suspended in their operation till his Assent should be obtained; and when so suspended, he has utterly neglected to attend to them.

He has refused to pass other Laws for the accommodation of large districts of people, unless those people would relinquish the right of Representation in the Legislature, a right inestimable to them and formidable to tyrants only. He has called together legislative bodies at places unusual, uncomfortable, and distant from the depository of their public Records, for the sole purpose of fatiguing them into compliance with his measures. He has dissolved Representative Houses repeatedly, for opposing with manly firmness his invasions on the rights of the people.

He has refused for a long time, after such dissolutions, to cause others to be elected; whereby the Legislative powers, incapable of Annihilation, have returned to the People at large for their exercise; the State remaining in the mean time exposed to all the dangers of invasion from without, and convulsions within.

He has endeavoured to prevent the population of these States; for that purpose obstructing the Laws for Naturalization of Foreigners; refusing to pass others to encourage their migrations hither, and raising the conditions of new Appropriations of Lands.

He has obstructed the Administration of Justice, by refusing his Assent to Laws for establishing Judiciary powers.

He has made Judges dependent on his Will alone, for the tenure of their offices, and the amount and payment of their salaries.

He has erected a multitude of New Offices, and sent hither swarms of Officers to harrass our people, and eat out their substance.

He has kept among us, in times of peace, Standing Armies without the Consent of our legislatures.

He has affected to render the Military independent of and superior to the Civil power.

He has combined with others to subject us to a jurisdiction foreign to our constitution, and unacknowledged by our laws; giving his Assent to their Acts of pretended Legislation:

For Quartering large bodies of armed troops among us:

For protecting them, by a mock Trial, from punishment for any Murders which they should commit on the Inhabitants of these States:

For cutting off our Trade with all parts of the world:

For imposing Taxes on us without our Consent: For depriving us in many cases, of the benefits of Trial by Jury:

For transporting us beyond Seas to be tried for pretended offences

For abolishing the free System of English Laws in a neighbouring Province, establishing therein an Arbitrary government, and enlarging its Boundaries so as to render it at once an example and fit instrument for introducing the same absolute rule into these Colonies:

For taking away our Charters, abolishing our most valuable Laws, and altering fundamentally the Forms of our Governments:

For suspending our own Legislatures, and declaring themselves invested with power to legislate for us in all cases whatsoever.

He has abdicated Government here, by declaring us out of his Protection and waging War against us. He has plundered our seas, ravaged our Coasts, burnt our towns, and destroyed the lives of our people.

He is at this time transporting large Armies of foreign Mercenaries to compleat the works of death, desolation and tyranny, already begun with circumstances of Cruelty & perfidy scarcely paralleled in the most barbarous ages, and totally unworthy the Head of a civilized nation.

He has constrained our fellow Citizens taken Captive on the high Seas to bear Arms against their Country, to become the executioners of their friends and Brethren, or to fall themselves by their Hands. He has excited domestic insurrections amongst us, and has endeavoured to bring on the inhabitants of our frontiers, the merciless Indian Savages, whose known rule of warfare, is an undistinguished destruction of all ages, sexes and conditions.

In every stage of these Oppressions We have Petitioned for Redress in the most humble terms: Our repeated Petitions have been answered only by repeated injury. A Prince whose character is thus marked by every act which may define a Tyrant, is unfit to be the ruler of a free people.

Nor have We been wanting in attentions to our Brittish brethren. We have warned them from time to time of attempts by their legislature to extend an unwarrantable jurisdiction over us. We have reminded them of the circumstances of our emigration and settlement here. We have appealed to their native justice and magnanimity, and we have conjured them by the ties of our common kindred to disavow these usurpations, which, would inevitably interrupt our connections and correspondence. They too have been deaf to the voice of justice and of consanguinity. We must, therefore, acquiesce in the necessity, which denounces our Separation, and hold them, as we hold the rest of mankind, Enemies in War, in Peace Friends.

We, therefore, the Representatives of the united States of America, in General Congress, Assembled, appealing to the Supreme Judge of the world for the rectitude of our intentions, do, in the Name, and by Authority of the good People of these Colonies, solemnly publish and declare, That these United Colonies are, and of Right ought to be Free and Independent States; that they are Absolved from all Allegiance to the British Crown, and that all political connection between them and the State of Great Britain, is and ought to be totally dissolved; and that as Free and Independent States, they have full Power to levy War, conclude Peace, contract Alliances, establish Commerce, and to do all other Acts and Things which Independent States may of right do. And for the support of this Declaration, with a firm reliance on the protection of divine Providence, we mutually pledge to each other our Lives, our Fortunes and our sacred Honor.

AMERICA'S SECOND DECLARATION OF INDEPENDENCE

AMERICA'S SECOND DECLARATION OF INDEPENDENCE

When in the course of human events, it becomes necessary for one people to dissolve the hatred bonds which have separated them from each other, and to assume, among the powers of the earth, the separate and equal stations to which the laws of nature and of Nature's God entitle them, a descent respect to the opinions of mankind requires that they should declare the causes which impel them to their misunderstanding.

We hold these truths to be self evident, that all men are created equal; that they are endowed by their Creator with certain inalienable rights; that among these, are life, liberty, and the pursuit of happiness. The history of the Caucasian American is a history of repeated injuries and usurpations, all having, in direct object, the establishment of an absolute tyranny over these people. To prove this, let facts be submitted to a candid world:

You have refused us accent to laws which would treat Blacks as equals in the bar room of justice.

You have forbidden Blacks from sharing in the blessings which they yearn for daily.

You have refused to pass other laws that would prohibit insults and injuries to your Black countrymen.

You have called together legislative bodies to block all paths to first class citizenship for Black Americans.

You have dissolved representative houses which had Black representatives during the Reconstruction era.

You have refused to cause others to be elected by padding ballot boxes in many parts of the country.

You have endeavored to prevent the Black from exercising his basic Rights.

You have obstructed the administration of justice by establishing one set of Laws for White who commit crimes and another set of Laws for Black who commit crimes.

You have made judges dependent on their will alone because most judges are appointed rather than elected to their powerful positions. You have erected a multitude of new offices to enable White Americans to keep Black Americans in an ancillary status.

You have kept among us "Uncle Toms" and "Aunt Nellies" and standing armies of Rebellious Racists to thwart our strides toward freedom.

You have affected to render laws of White supremacy superior to the laws embraced by the Bill of Rights.

You have combined intimidation and force to subject a jurisdiction foreign to our constitution.

a) For quartering large bodies of rarely-trained, actually-sick "policemen" to watch over us.

b) For protecting them by a Mock trial, from punishment, for ANY murders which they should commit on the inhabitants of these persons.

c) For cutting our trade with First-Class business by giving us Third-Class and Fourth-Class earning power.

d) For imposing First-Class taxes on us and giving us last-Class citizenship.

e) For depriving us, in many cases, of the benefit of trial by jury AND, in far too many cases, NO TRIAL AT ALL.

f) For transporting us from a small slum to a larger slum to avoid giving us the opportunity to earn the salary for the purpose of obtaining decent housing for our families.

g) For transporting us from a small slum to a larger slum to avoid giving us the opportunity to earn the salary for the purpose of obtaining decent housing for our families.

h) For abolishing the commitment, during the period of Reconstruction, which could have solved the racial problems many years ago.

i) For suspending our Rights and declaring themselves invested with power to legislate for us in all cases whatsoever.

j) You have abdicated Justice in all cases involving Black Americans.

k) You are, at this time, attempting to reword the other important historical documents and to work for more promises more tokenism, and more tyranny, already begun, with circumstance of cruelty and perfidy scarcely parallel in the most-barbarous ages, and totally unworthy the head of a civilized nation.

l) You have constrained our fellow citizens in all walks of public life.

m) You have excited domestic insurrections among us and have caused our trust, faith and hope to diminish as a result of same.

In every state of these oppressions, we have petitioned for redress, in the most humble terms, our repeated petitions have been answered only by repeated injury. A prince whose character is thus marked by every act which may define a tyrant is unfit to be the ruler of a free people.

We have warned them. We have reminded them. We have appealed to their native justice. We have conjured them. They, too, have been deaf to the voice of Justice and Righteousness. We must, therefore, acquiesce in the necessity which denounces our misunderstandings, and hold them, as we hold the rest of mankind, enemies in war, in peace, friends.

We, therefore, the blacks of the United States of America, in general Agreement, appealing to the Supreme Judge of the world for the rectitude of our intentions, do, in the name and by the authority of the good people of this country, solemnly publish and declare, that these people are, and of right ought to be, free and independent; that they are absolved from a subservient status, and that all misunderstandings between them and the Caucasians of the United States is, and ought to be, totally resolved; and that as free and independent persons, they have full RIGHTS to the ballot, to decent housing, to petition their leaders for redress of grievances without intimidation or fear, to marry whomever they choose, and to do all other acts and things which independent persons may of right do. And, for the support of this declaration, with a firm reliance on the protection of Divine Providence, we mutually pledge to each other our lives, our fortunes and our sacred honor.

CONCERNED BLACKS WHO LIVE IN AMERICA

RULES FOR LIVING IN A DEMOCRATIC SOCIETY

One cannot play the game of basketball with rules that were specifically written for the games of football, baseball or golf.

For me, the Constitution of the United States of America and its Amendments represent the rules for the game called "Democracy."

Furthermore, I firmly believe that the rules drafted for a democratic society is to make certain that one's rights and privileges will never infringe upon the rights and privileges of others.

THE CONSTITUTION OF THE UNITED STATES OF AMERICA

We the People of the United States, in Order to form a more perfect Union, establish Justice, insure domestic Tranquility, provide for the common defense, promote the general Welfare, and secure the Blessings of Liberty to ourselves and our Posterity, do ordain and establish this Constitution for the United States of America.

Article I

Section 1. All legislative Powers herein granted shall be vested in a Congress of the United States, which shall consist of a Senate and House of Representatives.

Section 2. The House of Representatives shall be composed of Members chosen every second Year by the People of the several States, and the Electors in each State shall have the Qualifications requisite for Electors of the most numerous Branch of the State Legislature.

No Person shall be a Representative who shall not have attained to the age of twenty five Years, and been seven Years a Citizen of the United States, and who shall not, when elected, be an Inhabitant of that State in which he shall be chosen.

Representatives and direct Taxes shall be apportioned among the several States which may be included within this Union, according to their respective Numbers, which shall be determined by adding to the whole Number of free Persons, including those bound to Service for a Term of Years, and excluding Indians not taxed, three fifths of all other

Persons. The actual Enumeration shall be made within three Years after the first Meeting of the Congress of the United States, and within every subsequent Term of ten Years, in such Manner as they shall by Law direct. The Number of Representatives shall not exceed one for every thirty Thousand, but each State shall have at Least one Representative; and until such enumeration shall be made, the State of New Hampshire shall be entitled to chuse three, Massachusetts eight, Rhode-Island and Providence Plantations one, Connecticut five, New-York six, New Jersey four, Pennsylvania eight, Delaware one, Maryland six, Virginia ten, North Carolina five, South Carolina five, and Georgia three.

When vacancies happen in the Representation from any State, the Executive Authority thereof shall issue Writs of Election to fill such Vacancies.

The House of Representatives shall chuse their Speaker and other Officers; and shall have the sole Power of Impeachment.

Section 3. The Senate of the United States shall be composed of two Senators from each State, chosen by the Legislature thereof, for six Years; and each Senator shall have one Vote.

Immediately after they shall be assembled in Consequence of the first Election, they shall be divided as equally as may be into three Classes. The Seats of the Senators of the first Class shall be vacated at the Expiration of the second Year, of the second Class at the Expiration of the fourth Year, and the third Class at the Expiration of the sixth Year, so that one third may be chosen every second Year; and if Vacancies happen by Resignation, or otherwise, during the Recess of the Legislature of any State, the Executive thereof may make temporary Appointments until the next Meeting of the Legislature, which shall then fill such Vacancies.

No Person shall be a Senator who shall not have attained to the Age of thirty Years, and been nine Years a Citizen of the United States and who shall not, when elected, be an Inhabitant of that State for which he shall be chosen.

The Vice President of the United States shall be President of the Senate, but shall have no Vote, unless they be equally divided.

The Senate shall chuse their other Officers, and also a President pro tempore, in the Absence of the Vice President, or when he shall exercise the Office of President of the United States.

The Senate shall have the sole Power to try all Impeachments. When sitting for that Purpose, they shall be on Oath or Affirmation. When the President of the United States is tried, the Chief Justice shall preside: And no Person shall be convicted without the Concurrence of two thirds of the Members present.

Judgment in Cases of Impeachment shall not extend further than to removal from Office, and disqualification to hold and enjoy any Office of Honor, Trust or Profit under the United States: but the Party convicted shall nevertheless be liable and subject to Indictment, Trial, Judgment and Punishment, according to Law.

Section 4. The Times, Places and Manner of holding Elections for Senators and Representatives, shall be prescribed in each State by the Legislature thereof; but the Congress may at any time by Law make or alter such Regulations, except as to the Places of chusing Senators.

The Congress shall assemble at least once in every Year, and such Meeting shall be on the first Monday in December, unless they shall by Law appoint a different Day.

Section 5. Each House shall be the Judge of the Elections, Returns and Qualifications of its own Members, and a Majority of each shall constitute a Quorum to do Business; but a smaller Number may adjourn from day to day, and may be authorized to compel the Attendance of absent Members, in such Manner, and under such Penalties as each House may provide.

Each House may determine the Rules of its Proceedings, punish its Members for disorderly Behaviour, and, with the Concurrence of two thirds, expel a Member.

Each House shall keep a Journal of its Proceedings, and from time to time publish the same, excepting such Parts as may in their Judgment require Secrecy; and the Yeas and Nays of the Members of either House on any question shall, at the Desire of one fifth of those Present, be entered on the Journal.

Neither House, during the Session of Congress, shall, without the Consent of the other, adjourn for more than three days, nor to any other Place than that in which the two Houses shall be sitting.

Section 6. The Senators and Representatives shall receive a Compensation for their Services, to be ascertained by Law, and paid out of the Treasury of the United States. They shall in all Cases, except Treason, Felony and Breach of the Peace, be privileged from Arrest during their Attendance at the Session of their respective Houses, and in going to and returning from the same; and for any Speech or Debate in either House, they shall not be questioned in any other Place.

No Senator or Representative shall, during the Time for which he was elected, be appointed to any civil Office under the Authority of the United States, which shall have been created, or the Emoluments whereof shall have been encreased during such time: and no Person holding any Office under the United States, shall be a Member of either House during his Continuance in Office.

Section 7. All Bills for raising Revenue shall originate in the House of Representatives; but the Senate may propose or concur with Amendments as on other Bills.

Every Bill which shall have passed the House of Representatives and the Senate, shall, before it become a Law, be presented to the President of the United States; if he approve he shall sign it, but if not he shall return it, with his Objections to that House in which it shall have originated, who shall enter the Objections at large on their Journal, and proceed to reconsider it. If after such Reconsideration two thirds of that House shall agree to pass the Bill, it shall be sent, together with the Objections, to the other House, by which it shall likewise be reconsidered, and if approved by two thirds of that House, it shall become a Law. But in all such Cases the Votes of both Houses shall be determined by Yeas and Nays, and the Names of the Persons voting for and against the Bill shall be entered on the Journal of each House respectively. If any Bill shall not be returned by the President within ten Days (Sundays excepted) after it shall have been presented to him, the Same shall be a Law, in like Manner as if he had signed it, unless the Congress by their Adjournment prevent its Return, in which Case it shall not be a Law.

Every Order, Resolution, or Vote to which the Concurrence of the Senate and House of Representatives may be necessary (except on a question of Adjournment) shall be presented to the President of the United States; and before the Same shall take Effect, shall be approved by him, or being disapproved by him, shall be repassed by two thirds of the Senate and House of Representatives, according to the Rules and Limitations prescribed in the Case of a Bill.

Section 8. The Congress shall have Power To lay and collect Taxes, Duties, Imposts and Excises, to pay the Debts and provide for the common Defence and general Welfare of the United States; but all Duties, Imposts and Excises shall be uniform throughout the United States;

To borrow Money on the credit of the United States;

To regulate Commerce with foreign Nations, and among the several States, and with the Indian Tribes;

To establish an uniform Rule of Naturalization, and uniform Laws on the subject of Bankruptcies throughout the United States;

To coin Money, regulate the Value thereof, and of foreign Coin, and fix the Standard of Weights and Measures;

To provide for the Punishment of counterfeiting the Securities and current Coin of the United States;

To establish Post Offices and post Roads;

To promote the Progress of Science and useful Arts, by securing for limited Times to Authors and Inventors the exclusive Right to their respective Writings and Discoveries;

To constitute Tribunals inferior to the supreme Court;

To define and punish Piracies and Felonies committed on the high Seas, and Offences against the Law of Nations;

To declare War, grant Letters of Marque and Reprisal, and make Rules concerning Captures on Land and Water;

To raise and support Armies, but no Appropriation of Money to that Use shall be for a longer Term than two Years;

To provide and maintain a Navy;

To make Rules for the Government and Regulation of the land and naval Forces;

To provide for calling forth the Militia to execute the Laws of the Union, suppress Insurrections and repel Invasions;

To provide for organizing, arming, and disciplining, the Militia, and for governing such Part of them as may be employed in the Service of the United States, reserving to the States respectively, the Appointment of the Officers, and the Authority of training the Militia according to the discipline prescribed by Congress;

To exercise exclusive Legislation in all Cases whatsoever, over such District (not exceeding ten Miles square) as may, by Cession of particular States, and the Acceptance of Congress, become the Seat of the Government of the United States, and to exercise like Authority over all Places purchased by the Consent of the Legislature of the State in which the Same shall be, for the Erection of Forts, Magazines, Arsenals, dock-Yards, and other needful Buildings;—And

To make all Laws which shall be necessary and proper for carrying into Execution the foregoing Powers, and all other Powers vested by this Constitution in the Government of the United States, or in any Department or Officer thereof.

Section 9. The Migration or Importation of such Persons as any of the States now existing shall think proper to admit, shall not be prohibited by the Congress prior to the Year one thousand eight hundred and eight, but a Tax or duty may be imposed on such Importation, not exceeding ten dollars for each Person.

    The Privilege of the Writ of Habeas Corpus shall not be suspended, unless when in Cases of Rebellion or Invasion the public Safety may require it.

    No Bill of Attainder or ex post facto Law shall be passed.

    No Capitation, or other direct, Tax shall be laid, unless in Proportion to the Census or Enumeration herein before directed to be taken.

No Tax or Duty shall be laid on Articles exported from any State.

No Preference shall be given by any Regulation of Commerce or Revenue to the Ports of one State over those of another: nor shall Vessels bound to, or from, one State, be obliged to enter, clear or pay Duties in another.

No Money shall be drawn from the Treasury, but in Consequence of Appropriations made by Law; and a regular Statement and Account of Receipts and Expenditures of all public Money shall be published from time to time.

No Title of Nobility shall be granted by the United States: And no Person holding any Office of Profit or Trust under them, shall, without the Consent of the Congress, accept of any present, Emolument, Office, or Title, of any kind whatever, from any King, Prince, or foreign State.

Section 10. No State shall enter into any Treaty, Alliance, or Confederation; grant Letters of Marque and Reprisal; coin Money; emit Bills of Credit; make any Thing but gold and silver Coin a Tender in Payment of Debts; pass any Bill of Attainder, ex post facto Law, or Law impairing the Obligation of Contracts, or grant any Title of Nobility.

No State shall, without the Consent of the Congress, lay any Imposts or Duties on Imports or Exports, except what may be absolutely necessary for executing it's inspection Laws: and the net Produce of all Duties and Imposts, laid by any State on Imports or Exports, shall be for the Use of the Treasury of the United States; and all such Laws shall be subject to the Revision and Controul of the Congress.

No State shall, without the Consent of Congress, lay any Duty of Tonnage, keep Troops, or Ships of War in time of Peace, enter into any Agreement or Compact with another State, or with a foreign Power, or engage in War, unless actually invaded, or in such imminent Danger as will not admit of delay.

Article II

Section 1. The executive Power shall be vested in a President of the United States of America. He shall hold his Office during the Term of four Years, and, together with the Vice President, chosen for the same Term, be elected, as follows:

Each State shall appoint, in such Manner as the Legislature thereof may direct, a Number of Electors, equal to the whole Number of Senators and Representatives to which the State may be entitled in the Congress: but no Senator or Representative, or Person holding an Office of Trust or Profit under the United States, shall be appointed an Elector.

The Electors shall meet in their respective States, and vote by Ballot for two Persons, of whom one at least shall not be an Inhabitant of the same State with themselves. And they shall make a List of all the Persons voted for, and of the Number of Votes for each; which List they shall sign and certify, and transmit sealed to the Seat of the Government of the United States, directed to the President of the Senate. The President of the Senate shall, in the Presence of the Senate and House of Representatives, open all the Certificates, and the Votes shall then be counted. The Person having the greatest Number of Votes shall be the President, if such Number be a Majority of the whole Number of Electors appointed; and if there be more than one who have such Majority, and have an equal Number of Votes, then the House of Representatives shall immediately chuse by Ballot one of them for President; and if no Person have a Majority, then from the five highest on the List the said House shall in like Manner chuse the President. But in chusing the President, the Votes shall be taken by States, the Representation from each State having one Vote; A quorum for this Purpose shall consist of a Member or Members from two thirds of the States, and a Majority of all the States shall be necessary to a Choice. In every Case, after the Choice of the President, the Person having the greatest Number of Votes of the Electors shall be the Vice President. But if there should remain two or more who have equal Votes, the Senate shall chuse from them by Ballot the Vice President.

The Congress may determine the Time of chusing the Electors, and the Day on which they shall give their Votes; which Day shall be the same throughout the United States.

No Person except a natural born Citizen, or a Citizen of the United States, at the time of the Adoption of this Constitution, shall be eligible to the Office of President; neither shall any Person be eligible to that Office who shall not have attained to the Age of thirty five Years, and been fourteen Years a Resident within the United States.

In Case of the Removal of the President from Office, or of his Death, Resignation, or Inability to discharge the Powers and Duties of the said Office, the Same shall devolve on the Vice President, and the Congress may by Law provide for the Case of Removal, Death, Resignation or

Inability, both of the President and Vice President, declaring what Officer shall then act as President, and such Officer shall act accordingly, until the Disability be removed, or a President shall be elected.

The President shall, at stated Times, receive for his Services, a Compensation, which shall neither be encreased nor diminished during the Period for which he shall have been elected, and he shall not receive within that Period any other Emolument from the United States, or any of them.

Before he enter on the Execution of his Office, he shall take the following Oath or Affirmation:—"I do solemnly swear (or affirm) that I will faithfully execute the Office of President of the United States, and will to the best of my Ability, preserve, protect and defend the Constitution of the United States."

Section 2. The President shall be Commander in Chief of the Army and Navy of the United States, and of the Militia of the several States, when called into the actual Service of the United States; he may require the Opinion, in writing, of the principal Officer in each of the executive Departments, upon any Subject relating to the Duties of their respective Offices, and he shall have Power to grant Reprieves and Pardons for Offences against the United States, except in Cases of Impeachment.

He shall have Power, by and with the Advice and Consent of the Senate, to make Treaties, provided two thirds of the Senators present concur; and he shall nominate, and by and with the Advice and Consent of the Senate, shall appoint Ambassadors, other public Ministers and Consuls, Judges of the supreme Court, and all other Officers of the United States, whose Appointments are not herein otherwise provided for, and which shall be established by Law: but the Congress may by Law vest the Appointment of such inferior Officers, as they think proper, in the President alone, in the Courts of Law, or in the Heads of Departments.

The President shall have Power to fill up all Vacancies that may happen during the Recess of the Senate, by granting Commissions which shall expire at the End of their next Session.

Section 3. He shall from time to time give to the Congress Information of the State of the Union, and recommend to their Consideration such Measures as he shall judge necessary and expedient; he may, on extraordinary Occasions, convene both Houses, or either of them, and in Case of Disagreement between them, with Respect to the Time of Adjournment, he may adjourn them to such Time as he shall think proper; he shall receive Ambassadors and other public Ministers; he shall take Care that the Laws be faithfully executed, and shall Commission all the Officers of the United States.

Section 4. The President, Vice President and all civil Officers of the United States, shall be removed from Office on Impeachment for, and Conviction of, Treason, Bribery, or other high Crimes and Misdemeanors.

Article III

Section 1. The judicial Power of the United States, shall be vested in one supreme Court, and in such inferior Courts as the Congress may from time to time ordain and establish. The Judges, both of the supreme and inferior Courts, shall hold their Offices during good Behaviour, and shall, at stated Times, receive for their Services, a Compensation, which shall not be diminished during their Continuance in Office.

Section 2. The judicial Power shall extend to all Cases, in Law and Equity, arising under this Constitution, the Laws of the United States, and Treaties made, or which shall be made, under their Authority;—to all Cases affecting Ambassadors, other public Ministers and Consuls;—to all Cases of admiralty and maritime Jurisdiction;—to Controversies to which the United States shall be a Party;—to Controversies between two or more States;—between a State and Citizens of another State;—between Citizens of different States;—between Citizens of the same State claiming Lands under Grants of different States, and between a State, or the Citizens thereof, and foreign States, Citizens or Subjects.

In all Cases affecting Ambassadors, other public Ministers and Consuls, and those in which a State shall be Party, the supreme Court shall have original Jurisdiction. In all the other Cases before mentioned, the supreme Court shall have appellate Jurisdiction, both as to Law and Fact, with such Exceptions, and under such Regulations as the Congress shall make.

The Trial of all Crimes, except in Cases of Impeachment, shall be by Jury; and such Trial shall be held in the State where the said Crimes shall have been committed; but when not committed within any State, the Trial shall be at such Place or Places as the Congress may by Law have directed.

Section 3. Treason against the United States, shall consist only in levying War against them, or in adhering to their Enemies, giving them Aid and Comfort. No Person shall be convicted of Treason unless on the Testimony of two Witnesses to the same overt Act, or on Confession in open Court.

The Congress shall have Power to declare the Punishment of Treason, but no Attainder of Treason shall work Corruption of Blood, or Forfeiture except during the Life of the Person attainted.

Article IV

Section 1. Full Faith and Credit shall be given in each State to the public Acts, Records, and judicial Proceedings of every other State. And the Congress may by general Laws prescribe the Manner in which such Acts, Records, and Proceedings shall be proved, and the Effect thereof.

Section 2. The Citizens of each State shall be entitled to all Privileges and Immunities of Citizens in the several States.

A Person charged in any State with Treason, Felony, or other Crime, who shall flee from Justice, and be found in another State, shall on Demand of the executive Authority of the State from which he fled, be delivered up, to be removed to the State having Jurisdiction of the Crime.

No Person held to Service or Labour in one State, under the Laws thereof, escaping into another, shall, in Consequence of any Law or Regulation therein, be discharged from such Service or Labour, but shall be delivered up on Claim of the Party to whom such Service or Labour may be due.

Section 3. New States may be admitted by the Congress into this Union; but no new States shall be formed or erected within the Jurisdiction of any other State; nor any State be formed by the Junction of two or more States, or Parts of States, without the Consent of the Legislatures of the States concerned as well as of the Congress.

The Congress shall have Power to dispose of and make all needful Rules and Regulations respecting the Territory or other Property belonging to the United States; and nothing in this Constitution shall be so construed as to Prejudice any Claims of the United States, or of any particular State.

Section 4. The United States shall guarantee to every State in this Union a Republican Form of Government, and shall protect each of them against Invasion; and on Application of the Legislature, or of the Executive (when the Legislature cannot be convened) against domestic Violence.

Article V

The Congress, whenever two thirds of both Houses shall deem it necessary, shall propose Amendments to this Constitution, or, on the Application of the Legislatures of two thirds of the several States, shall call a Convention for proposing Amendments, which, in either Case, shall be valid to all Intents and Purposes, as Part of this Constitution, when ratified by the Legislatures of three fourths of the several States, or by Conventions in three fourths thereof, as the one or the other Mode of Ratification may be proposed by the Congress; Provided that no Amendment which may be made prior to the Year One thousand eight hundred and eight shall in any Manner affect the first and fourth Clauses in the Ninth Section of the first Article; and that no State, without its Consent, shall be deprived of its equal Suffrage in the Senate.

Article IV

All Debts contracted and Engagements entered into, before the Adoption of this Constitution, shall be as valid against the United States under this Constitution, as under the Confederation.

This Constitution, and the Laws of the United States which shall be made in Pursuance thereof; and all Treaties made, or which shall be made, under the Authority of the United States, shall be the supreme Law of the Land; and the Judges in every State shall be bound thereby, any Thing in the Constitution or Laws of any State to the Contrary notwith-standing.

The Senators and Representatives before mentioned, and the Members of the several State Legislatures, and all executive and judicial Officers, both of the United States and of the several States, shall be bound by Oath or Affirmation, to support this Constitution; but no religious Test shall ever be required as a Qualification to any Office or public Trust under the United States.

Article VII

The Ratification of the Conventions of nine States, shall be sufficient for the Establishment of this Constitution between the States so ratifying the Same.

Done in Convention by the Unanimous Consent of the States present the Seventeenth Day of September in the Year of our Lord one thousand seven hundred and Eighty seven and of the Independence of the United States of America the Twelfth

In witness whereof We have hereunto subscribed our Names,

George Washington—President and deputy from Virginia

New Hampshire: John Langdon, Nicholas Gilman

Massachusetts: Nathaniel Gorham, Rufus King

Connecticut: William Samuel Johnson, Roger Sherman

New York: Alexander Hamilton

New Jersey: William Livingston, David Brearly, William Paterson, Jonathan Dayton

Pennsylvania: Benjamin Franklin, Thomas Mifflin, Robert Morris, George Clymer, Thomas FitzSimons, Jared Ingersoll, James Wilson, Gouverneur Morris

Delaware: George Read, Gunning Bedford, Jr., John Dickinson, Richard Bassett, Jacob Broom

Maryland: James McHenry, Daniel of Saint Thomas Jenifer, Daniel Carroll

Virginia: John Blair, James Madison, Jr.

North Carolina: William Blount, Richard Dobbs Spaight, Hugh Williamson

South Carolina: John Rutledge, Charles Cotesworth Pinckney, Charles Pinckney, Pierce Butler

Georgia: William Few, Abraham Baldwin

THE FIRST 10 AMENDMENTS

(Bill of Rights)

THE AMENDMENTS NOTE

The following are the Amendments to the Constitution. The first ten Amendments collectively are commonly known as the *Bill of Rights. History*

Amendment 1—Freedom of Religion, Press, *Expression. Ratified* 12/15/1791. *Note*

Congress shall make no law respecting an establishment of religion, or prohibiting the free exercise thereof; or abridging the freedom of speech, or of the press; or the right of the people peaceably to assemble, and to petition the Government for a *redress* of grievances.

Amendment 2—Right to Bear Arms. *Ratified* 12/15/1791. *Note*

A well regulated Militia, being necessary to the security of a free State, the right of the people to keep and bear Arms, shall not be *infringed.*

Amendment 3—Quartering of Soldiers. *Ratified* 12/15/1791. *Note*

No Soldier shall, in time of peace be *quartered* in any house, without the consent of the Owner, nor in time of war, but in a manner to be prescribed by law.

Amendment 4—Search and Seizure. *Ratified* 12/15/1791.

The right of the people to be secure in their persons, houses, papers, and effects, against unreasonable searches and seizures, shall not be violated, and no Warrants shall issue, but upon probable cause, supported by Oath or affirmation, and particularly describing the place to be searched, and the persons or things to be seized.

Amendment 5—Trial and Punishment, Compensation for Takings. *Ratified* 12/15/1791.

No person shall be held to answer for a capital, or otherwise infamous crime, unless on a presentment or indictment of a Grand Jury, except in cases arising in the land or naval forces, or in the Militia, when in actual service in time of War or public danger; nor shall any person *be subject for the same offense to be twice put in jeopardy of life or limb*; nor shall be compelled in any criminal case to be a witness against himself, nor be *deprived* of life, liberty, or property, without *due process* of law; nor shall private property be taken for public use, without just compensation.

Amendment 6—Right to Speedy Trial, Confrontation of Witnesses. *Ratified* 12/15/1791.

In all criminal prosecutions, the accused shall enjoy the right to a speedy and public trial, by an *impartial* jury of the State and district wherein the crime shall have been committed, which district shall have been previously ascertained by law, and to be informed of the nature and cause of the accusation; to be confronted with the witnesses against him; to have compulsory process for obtaining witnesses in his favor, and to have the Assistance of Counsel for his *defence*.

Amendment 7—Trial by Jury in Civil Cases. *Ratified* 12/15/1791.

In Suits at common law, where the value in controversy shall exceed twenty dollars, the right of trial by jury shall be preserved, and no fact tried by a jury, shall be otherwise re-examined in any Court of the United States, than according to the rules of the common law.

Amendment 8—Cruel and Unusual Punishment. *Ratified* 12/15/1791.

Excessive bail shall not be required, nor excessive fines imposed, nor cruel and unusual punishments inflicted.

Amendment 9—Construction of Constitution. *Ratified* 12/15/1791.

The *enumeration* in the Constitution, of certain rights, shall not be construed to deny or disparage others retained by the people.

Amendment 10—Powers of the States and People. *Ratified* 12/15/1791. *Note*

The powers not delegated to the United States by the Constitution, nor prohibited by it to the States, are reserved to the States respectively, or to the people.

Amendment 11—Judicial Limits. *Ratified* 2/7/1795. *Note History*

The Judicial power of the United States shall not be construed to extend to any suit in law or equity, commenced or prosecuted against one of the United States by Citizens of another State, or by Citizens or Subjects of any Foreign State.

Amendment 12—Choosing the President, Vice-President. *Ratified 6/15/1804. Note History The Electoral College*

The Electors shall meet in their respective states, and vote by ballot for President and Vice-President, one of whom, at least, shall not be an inhabitant of the same state with themselves; they shall name in their ballots the person voted for as President, and in distinct ballots the person voted for as Vice-President, and they shall make distinct lists of all persons voted for as President, and of all persons voted for as Vice-President and of the number of votes for each, which lists they shall sign and certify, and transmit sealed to the seat of the government of the United States, directed to the President of the Senate;

The President of the Senate shall, in the presence of the Senate and House of Representatives, open all the certificates and the votes shall then be counted;

The person having the greatest Number of votes for President, shall be the President, if such number be a majority of the whole number of Electors appointed; and if no person have such majority, then from the persons having the highest numbers not exceeding three on the list of those voted for as President, the House of Representatives shall choose immediately, by ballot, the President. But in choosing the President, the votes shall be taken by states, the representation from each state having one vote; a *quorum* for this purpose shall consist of a member or members from two-thirds of the states, and a majority of all the states shall be necessary to a choice. And if the House of Representatives shall not choose a President whenever the right of choice shall devolve upon them, before the fourth day of March next following, then the Vice-President shall act as President, as in the case of the death or other constitutional disability of the President.

The person having the greatest number of votes as Vice-President, shall be the Vice-President, if such number be a majority of the whole number of Electors appointed, and if no person have a majority, then from the two highest numbers on the list, the Senate shall choose the Vice-President; a *quorum* for the purpose shall consist of two-thirds of the whole number of Senators, and a majority of the whole number shall be necessary to a choice. But no person constitutionally ineligible to the office of President shall be eligible to that of Vice-President of the United States.

Amendment 13—Slavery Abolished. *Ratified* 12/6/1865. *History*

1. Neither slavery nor involuntary servitude, except as a punishment for crime whereof the party shall have been duly convicted, shall exist within the United States, or any place subject to their *jurisdiction*.
2. Congress shall have power to enforce this article by appropriate legislation.

Amendment 14—Citizenship Rights. *Ratified* 7/9/1868. *Note History*

1. All persons born or naturalized in the United States, and subject to the *jurisdiction* thereof, are citizens of the United States and of the State wherein they reside. No State shall make or enforce any law which shall abridge the privileges or immunities of citizens of the United States; nor shall any State *deprive* any person of life, liberty, or property, without *due process* of law; nor deny to any person within its *jurisdiction* the equal protection of the laws.
2. Representatives shall be *apportioned* among the several States according to their respective numbers, counting the whole number of persons in each State, excluding Indians not taxed. But when the right to vote at any election for the choice of electors for President and Vice-President of the United States, Representatives in Congress, the Executive and Judicial officers of a State, or the members of the Legislature thereof, is denied to any of the male inhabitants of such State, being twenty-one years of age, and citizens of the United States, or in any way abridged, except for participation in rebellion, or other crime, the basis of representation therein shall be reduced in the proportion which the number of such male citizens shall bear to the whole number of male citizens twenty-one years of age in such State.
3. No person shall be a Senator or Representative in Congress, or elector of President and Vice-President, or hold any office, civil or

military, under the United States, or under any State, who, having previously taken an oath, as a member of Congress, or as an officer of the United States, or as a member of any State legislature, or as an executive or judicial officer of any State, to support the Constitution of the United States, shall have engaged in insurrection or rebellion against the same, or given aid or comfort to the enemies thereof. But Congress may by a vote of two-thirds of each House, remove such disability.

4. The validity of the public debt of the United States, authorized by law, including debts incurred for payment of pensions and bounties for services in suppressing insurrection or rebellion, shall not be questioned. But neither the United States nor any State shall assume or pay any debt or obligation incurred in aid of insurrection or rebellion against the United States, or any claim for the loss or emancipation of any slave; but all such debts, obligations and claims shall be held illegal and void.

5. The Congress shall have power to enforce, by appropriate legislation, the provisions of this article.

Amendment 15—Race No Bar to Vote. *Ratified* 2/3/1870. *History*

1. The right of citizens of the United States to vote shall not be denied or abridged by the United States or by any State on account of race, color, or previous condition of servitude.

2. The Congress shall have power to enforce this article by appropriate legislation.

Amendment 16—Status of Income Tax Clarified. *Ratified* 2/3/1913. *Note History*

The Congress shall have power to lay and collect taxes on incomes, from whatever source derived, without *apportionment* among the several States, and without regard to any census or *enumeration*.

Amendment 17—Senators Elected by Popular Vote. *Ratified* 4/8/1913. *History*

The Senate of the United States shall be composed of two Senators from each State, elected by the people thereof, for six years; and each Senator shall have one vote. The electors in each State shall have the qualifications requisite for electors of the most numerous branch of the State legislatures.

When vacancies happen in the representation of any State in the Senate, the executive authority of such State shall issue writs of election to fill such vacancies: Provided, That the legislature of any State may empower the executive thereof to make temporary appointments until the people fill the vacancies by election as the legislature may direct.

This amendment shall not be so construed as to affect the election or term of any Senator chosen before it becomes valid as part of the Constitution.

Amendment 18—Liquor Abolished. *Ratified* 1/16/1919. Repealed by *Amendment 21*, 12/5/1933. *History*

1. After one year from the ratification of this article the manufacture, sale, or transportation of intoxicating liquors within, the importation thereof into, or the exportation thereof from the United States and all territory subject to the *jurisdiction* thereof for beverage purposes is hereby prohibited.
2. The Congress and the several States shall have concurrent power to enforce this article by appropriate legislation.
3. This article shall be inoperative unless it shall have been ratified as an amendment to the Constitution by the legislatures of the several States, as provided in the Constitution, within seven years from the date of the submission hereof to the States by the Congress.

Amendment 19—Women's *Suffrage*, *Ratified* 8/18/1920. *History*

The right of citizens of the United States to vote shall not be denied or abridged by the United States or by any State on account of sex.

Congress shall have power to enforce this article by appropriate legislation.

Amendment 20—Presidential, Congressional Terms. *Ratified* 1/23/1933. *History*

1. The terms of the President and Vice President shall end at noon on the 20th day of January, and the terms of Senators and Representatives at noon on the 3d day of January, of the years in which such terms would have ended if this article had not been ratified; and the terms of their successors shall then begin.
2. The Congress shall assemble at least once in every year, and such meeting shall begin at noon on the 3d day of January, unless they shall by law appoint a different day.
3. If, at the time fixed for the beginning of the term of the President, the President elect shall have died, the Vice President elect shall become President. If a President shall not have been chosen before the time fixed for the beginning of his term, or if the President elect shall have failed to qualify, then the Vice President elect shall act as President until a President shall have qualified; and the Congress may by law provide for the case wherein neither a President elect nor a Vice President elect shall have qualified, declaring who shall then act as President, or the manner in which one who is to act shall be selected, and such person shall act accordingly until a President or Vice President shall have qualified.
4. The Congress may by law provide for the case of the death of any of the persons from whom the House of Representatives may choose a President whenever the right of choice shall have developed upon them, and for the case of the death of any of the persons from whom the Senate may choose a Vice President whenever the right of choice shall have devolved upon them.
5. Sections 1 and 2 shall take effect on the 15th day of October following the ratification of this article.

6. This article shall be inoperative unless it shall have been ratified as an amendment to the Constitution by the legislatures of three-fourths of the several States within seven years from the date of its submission.

Amendment 21—*Amendment 18* Repealed. *Ratified* 12/5/1933. *History*

1. The eighteenth article of amendment to the Constitution of the United States is hereby repealed.
2. The transportation or importation into any State, Territory, or possession of the United States for delivery or use therein of intoxicating liquors, in violation of the laws thereof, is hereby prohibited.
3. The article shall be inoperative unless it shall have been ratified as an amendment to the Constitution by conventions in the several States, as provided in the Constitution, within seven years from the date of the submission hereof to the States by the Congress.

Amendment 22—Presidential Term Limits. *Ratified* 2/27/1951. *History*

1. No person shall be elected to the office of the President more than twice, and no person who has held the office of President, or acted as President, for more than two years of a term to which some other person was elected President shall be elected to the office of the President more than once. But this Article shall not apply to any person holding the office of President, when this Article was proposed by the Congress, and shall not prevent any person who may be holding the office of President, or acting as President, during the term within which this Article becomes operative from holding the office of President or acting as President during the remainder of such term.
2. This article shall be inoperative unless it shall have been ratified as an amendment to the Constitution by the legislatures of three-fourths of the several States within seven years from the date of its submission to the States by the Congress.

Amendment 23—Presidential Vote for District of Columbia. *Ratified* 3/29/1961. *History*

1. The District constituting the seat of Government of the United States shall appoint in such manner as the Congress may direct: A number of electors of President and Vice President equal to the whole number of Senators and Representatives in Congress to which the District would be entitled if it were a State, but in no event more than the least populous State; they shall be in addition to those appointed by the States, but they shall be considered, for the purposes of the election of President and Vice President, to be electors appointed by a State; and they shall meet in the District and perform such duties as provided by the twelfth article of amendment.
2. The Congress shall have power to enforce this article by appropriate legislation.

Amendment 24—*Poll Tax* Barred. *Ratified* 1/23/1964. *History*

1. The right of citizens of the United States to vote in any primary or other election for President or Vice President, for electors for President or Vice President, or for Senator or Representative in Congress, shall not be denied or abridged by the United States or any State by reason of failure to pay any *poll tax* or other tax.
2. The Congress shall have power to enforce this article by appropriate legislation.

Amendment 25—Presidential Disability and Succession. *Ratified* 2/10/1967. *Note History*

1. In case of the removal of the President from office or of his death or resignation, the Vice President shall become President.
2. Whenever there is a vacancy in the office of the Vice President, the President shall nominate a Vice President who shall take

office upon confirmation by a majority vote of both Houses of Congress.

3. Whenever the President transmits to the President pro tempore of the Senate and the Speaker of the House of Representatives his written declaration that he is unable to discharge the powers and duties of his office, and until he transmits to them a written declaration to the contrary, such powers and duties shall be discharged by the Vice President as Acting President.

4. Whenever the Vice President and a majority of either the principal officers of the executive departments or of such other body as Congress may by law provide, transmit to the President pro tempore of the Senate and the Speaker of the House of Representatives their written declaration that the President is unable to discharge the powers and duties of his office, the Vice President shall immediately assume the powers and duties of the office as Acting President.

Thereafter, when the President transmits to the President pro tempore of the Senate and the Speaker of the House of Representatives his written declaration that no inability exists, he shall resume the powers and duties of his office unless the Vice President and a majority of either the principal officers of the executive department or of such other body as Congress may by law provide, transmit within four days to the President pro tempore of the Senate and the Speaker of the House of Representatives their written declaration that the President is unable to discharge the powers and duties of his office. Thereupon Congress shall decide the issue, assembling within forty eight hours for that purpose if not in session. If the Congress, within twenty one days after receipt of the latter written declaration, or, if Congress is not in session, within twenty one days after Congress is required to assemble, determines by two thirds vote of both Houses that the President is unable to discharge the powers and duties of his office, the Vice President shall continue to discharge the same as Acting President; otherwise, the President shall resume the powers and duties of his office.

Amendment 26—Voting Age Set to 18 Years. *Ratified* 7/1/1971. *History*

1. The right of citizens of the United States, who are eighteen years of age or older, to vote shall not be denied or abridged by the United States or by any State on account of age.
2. The Congress shall have power to enforce this article by appropriate legislation.

Amendment 27—Limiting Congressional Pay Increases. *Ratified 5/7/1992. History*

No law, varying the compensation for the services of the Senators and Representatives, shall take effect, until an election of Representatives shall have intervened.

IT IS MY FIRM CONVICTION THAT ANY MAN WHO DENIES ME THAT WHICH HE WOULD DIE TO OBTAIN, PROTECT AND PRESERVE FOR HIMSELF DISPLAYS THE HIGHEST FORM OF HYPOCRISY.

Herman M. Witten, Sr.

THE VERDICT

(America's Trial For The Ages)

PRELUDE TO THE VERDICT

From my earliest childhood days, I have been somewhat confused as to why Black Americans were not, and are not today, treated as first class citizens in this great country. I did know, however, that something terribly-important must have happened quite early in our history.

Consequently, after much research, I have utilized a formula consisting of a little fiction and a great deal of truth to depict events that "occurred" long before now.

The Verdict was not written to embarrass Americans of Caucasian descent. I firmly believe that causing a state of self-conscious distress on the part of the contemporary Americans would prove to be counter productive.

It is my hope that these few pages of the printed word will, in some small way, give the reader a new look at America's historical past.

The Verdict is my conception of the "trial" that rendered the decision which restricted the freedom of all Black Americans in these "United" States.

It must be made crystal-clear that there is no law in America which states that its citizens of Negroid ancestry are to be ancillary human beings to any other race of people. I have seen no factual statements which support the theory that Black Americans are inferior persons, nor have I read from any authoritative source that these very citizens—of-color are inherently submissive. In other words, in my mind, there is no documentary evidence that can be found among America's most sacred writings which substantiates the "fact" that Black Americans are to be forever subjected to the state of perpetual enslavement.

I feel it is imperative that all persons come to understand that whenever anyone in America is apprehended, convicted and sentenced to life in prison for a given crime, there is usually a great possibility the offender, after a few years, can and may be set free depending upon his or her behavioral pattern. That is not true in the case of millions of Black Americans. These very people have been "convicted" and sentenced to life in "prison," without pardon, for a "crime" they did *not* commit.

Their "crime" was not treason, murder, rape, assault or even robbery. They were apprehended, booked, convicted and sentenced by "White" Americans for simply being the sons and the daughters of at least one or the other parent who happened to be of African heritage—a situation about which they had absolutely no control.

It was because of this harsh, ruthless and unforgiving penalty which was imposed upon all Black Americans that gave me the impetus to write *The Verdict*. This piece of writing can, henceforth and forevermore, be referred to as the "legal" document that officially certified the true status of all Black Americans in this so called "Democratic" country as "White" America had always intended for it to be.

THE VERDICT

I will never forget that day, for it was the 4th of July, and everyone was celebrating the Independence of this great country. A Special Delivery Messenger arrived at my front door with a telegram.

I opened the envelope and read these words:

> "ALL BLACKS IN AMERICA WILL STAND TRIAL ON THE 15TH DAY OF JULY, THIS YEAR, IN WASHINGTON, D.C. BEFORE A FEDERAL JUDGE IN ORDER THAT THEIR STATUS MIGHT BE DETERMINED AND TO ANSWER TO THE CHARGE—WHY THEY CHOSE TO BE BLACK!
>
> YOU ARE TO INFORM THE OTHER BLACKS IN THIS AREA."

I cannot begin to tell you the hurt that I experienced when I first read the telegram. My true feelings at that time seemed almost inexplicable. My entire body went limp, and my fingertips became numb. My heart began beating fast. My legs became weak, and my breathing was somewhat erratic. Sweat dripped from my forehead and mixed with the tears that filled my eyes. I was shocked and terrified. I was so confused until I just stood there in complete silence for several moments. Finally, I wiped away the tears and began gazing out the window as I pondered my next move.

The question that kept coming to my mind was, "What are the 'Whites' intending to do this time?" With my head in my hands, I said a lengthy but silent prayer before calling a few of my relatives and friends. I asked them to come to my home immediately and to bring others with them.

I called the best Constitutional lawyer in the country. After all, this was one case that we could not afford to lose. This lawyer was of Caucasian descent. He said that he would not take the case for fear of retaliation from his own people. I pleaded and begged him to change his mind. I was desperate! My people needed his services badly. I said to him that, as an American citizen himself, it was his *duty* to help alleviate human suffering among his fellow-brethren. He said, "NO!" and hung up the telephone. I was again hurt.

I called two other lawyers, but neither of them would talk to me. I was beginning to "get the message."

Soon thereafter, all of the Blacks that I had called arrived, and I wasted no time telling them about the telegram and the importance of the meeting. I told them about the difficulty that I had experienced trying to get legal representation.

We immediately engaged in a serious discussion about our plight, and at one point, an elderly gentleman rose and suggested that we choose from among ourselves one who could most aptly represent the Black American people. I was their choice. I did not wish to refuse this responsibility, but I informed them that I was not a lawyer, nor had I ever before had any legal experience. They told me that they had no one else to speak for them. After having heard this, I immediately accepted the challenge. It was now my responsibility to defend the whole of the Negroid race here in America.

I knew that I had nearly two weeks to prepare myself before the day of the trial, but how could anyone prove "Why he or she chose to be Black?" No one has a choice to be whoever and whatever he or she wants to be. Not even the ones who hold our fate in their hands have such a choice. I kept asking myself just how contemptuous and repulsive can a people become? Are such persons really human?

This was not the time to debate the inhumanity of the oppressors, but a time to act. This case was of such importance until the whole world had shown an interest. Representatives from each country on the face of the earth were to appear as living witnesses to this historic "trial."

I will never forget the day of that "trial," for it was such a beautiful day. The temperature was in the mid seventies. There was absolutely no breeze to interrupt the proceedings. I can recall seeing many Caucasians as they went about their daily chores, but the Black Americans were preparing themselves for the most important day of their entire lives as members of the human race.

The "trial" was to be held in this country's largest outdoor stadium that was located in its Capital city of Washington, D.C. This amphitheater had a seating capacity of more than six hundred thousand persons. It was oval in shape with one hundred tiers placed one above the other. To me, it resembled a large egg shaped bowl, and it was, perhaps, the largest piece of architecture ever constructed by man. It, alone, was a sight to behold!

The stage was situated at one narrow peak of this oval-shaped arena. The setting had the atmosphere of an indoor courtroom. There were special sections for the jurors, the press, the judge, the reporters and the other courtroom officials. There were microphones and loud speakers all over the place. There were signs which specified the sitting areas for all the foreign delegations, who were seated with the countries from their respective continents.

The "trial" was to begin at two o'clock p.m. All of my people arrived one hour earlier. They sat just to the left of the judge's bench. One-half hour prior to the start of the "trial," all of the delegations were seated and waiting. I was then escorted through that multitude of people by four large Caucasian men. I was made to stand just in front of my people and to face that huge gathering, which extended as far as I could possibly see.

The representatives from the continents of Africa, Asia and South America filled the balconies, and the delegations from the continents of Europe and North America occupied the main floor. I remember, quite vividly, seeing the representatives from Burma, Siam, China, India, Russia, Indonesia, Germany, Vietnam, Nigeria and Ghana.

The President of the "United States of America" and his cabinet sat just in front of me. The members of the Supreme Court were there too, and they were even dressed in their long black robes. What a beautiful sight! I must admit that this was the most colorful and the most dramatic spectacle that I had ever witnessed in all the years of my life. Never again will the eyes of man view so much beauty and pageantry as was seen on that one occasion.

Shortly, thereafter, the jurors began coming in and taking their seats. This jury consisted of twelve Caucasian men whose jobs ranged from that of a bank president to a member of one of America's hate groups. All seemed to be of middle age with austere and determined expressions on their faces.

There was a pause for about five minutes, with hardly anyone making a sound, before the Court Clerk rose to announce the entry of the judge. He said, "Ladies and Gentlemen, please rise—for now entering is the Honorable Jim Crow." All eyes were then focused on the one man who was to preside over this all-important case. I remember the judge as a tall, stately gentleman with solid white hair. He walked with a slight limp, and as soon as he had stationed himself, he hit his gavel upon the lectern and said, "This court is now in session."

The Court Clerk came forward and stood just in front of the judge's podium. He faced the delegations and made a few remarks. I do recall hearing him say, "The 'United' States of America versus all Black people. They are being charged with the following:

"THEY HAVE CHOSEN TO BE BLACK."

As soon as the Court Clerk had finished reading his statements, the judge asked if the Blacks had a spokesperson. Someone went to the judge and whispered a few words in his ear, and the judge nodded agreement and said, "very well, carry on."

Several procedural court room amenities were carried out before the prosecuting attorney took the floor. Some of the points that this prosecuting attorney mentioned are still vague in my mind, but I do remember him saying: (1) that Blacks were incapable of being educated, (2) that Black men constantly raped "White" women, (3) that the illegitimacy rate among Black women far exceeded that of "White" women, (4) that Blacks wanted to work in "White" people's jobs, (5) that Blacks wanted to live where "White" folks lived, (6) that Blacks wanted to eat in public places with "White" persons, (7) that Blacks wanted to be thought of as citizens of the "United" States of America, (8) that Blacks wanted the same "Rights" as "Whites," (9) that Blacks were extremely dirty, (10) that Blacks could not be trusted, (11) that Blacks would take a "mile if given an inch," and (12) that one day the Blacks would probably ask for complete freedom. He also presented many statistics to substantiate his remarks.

This prosecuting attorney, no doubt, was the very best that this country could possibly have chosen, for his arguments were highly persuasive. His lucid tongue and his smooth delivery, coupled with his unique presentation, would have convinced anyone that what he said was nothing short of the truth. I have never heard a man talk as he talked that day.

When the prosecuting attorney had finished, I was asked to take the stand on behalf of my people. I did, but first I was given an oral oath. As soon as I sat down, expecting to be questioned, the prosecuting attorney stood and said, "Your Honor, I find it unnecessary to ask the defendants' representative anything." I knew then that something was being taken for granted. The judge then turned to me and asked if I cared to refute any of the prosecuting attorney's charges. I was to show just cause why my people should not be found guilty of those very accusations.

I said, "Your Honor, I feel it would be superfluous for me to waste your time, my people's time, and the time of the thousands of distinguished dignitaries and visitors here by even commenting on those ridiculous charges that were stated by the prosecuting attorney. However, I will say that my people and I have always asked that all Americans, regardless of color, be treated equally. Any person who demands freedom for himself but who denies this very freedom for his fellow man exemplifies the greatest form of hypocrisy." I then walked back to my position just in front of my people.

Why, everyone seemed startled by my brief rebuttal. My people, too, seemed disappointed. They were terribly displeased. I felt uneasy. I felt as though I had let them down. The members of the delegations began to move about and talk out loud. The chatter became so turbulent until the judge had to ask for quiet. Just what happened next I don't know, but no one in the world felt as badly as I.

The next thing that I recall seeing was the prosecuting attorney walking over toward the jurors. He reiterated his earlier points with even more vigor and determination, and he told the members of that jury that they had no alternative but to render a verdict of guilty—without mercy.

When the prosecuting attorney had finished, I approached the jurors and said, "Gentlemen of the jury, we come not to antagonize you, but to beg of you mercy. We ask that you merely exchange places with us for the moment, and then make your decision.

I paused briefly to see the various facial expressions of each juror. Not one of them seemed as though he was listening to me. At that very instant, I was almost convinced that the verdict was predetermined. Nonetheless, I continued. "You men," I said, "must realize that you are our only hope. Please don't let us down". I then walked back to my people.

The judge lectured briefly to the jurors and asked that they do everything within their power to render a verdict on that day. The jurors left the "Court Room" to deliberate, and the judge declared a recess.

I cannot remember seeing any of the members of the various delegations leaving their seats. I do recall, however, witnessing many persons whispering and passing comments among themselves.

After but *ten* minutes of deliberating, the members of the jury returned and took their seats. Moments later, the judge re-appeared. I need not tell you about the apprehension and the anxiety that all of the Black-American people experienced at that time. Everyone was shocked to know that the jury had deliberated for no more than ten minutes. It was almost like a bad dream.

The judge asked whether or not the jury had reached a verdict. The chairman of the jury stood and said, "Yes, we have, Your Honor." The judge then asked all Black-Americans to stand and face the jury. Words alone cannot begin to describe the tenseness that was felt throughout the arena. I saw mothers embracing their children as tightly as they could. There were those who were holding their breath, and I was one of them. Some were looking upward for divine assistance. I noticed that the delegations from the Continent of Africa had begun to stand. Soon afterwards, delegation after delegation began standing out of respect for that all-important decision. Momentarily, you could not hear a sound anywhere. It was as though the world had stood still. I was frozen stiff with my eyes glued on the mouth of the Chairman of that jury, possibly, in hopes of finding out the verdict before anyone else simply by reading his lips. The judge then asked, "What is your verdict?" "Your Honor," the spokesman replied, "we find the defendants guilty as charged, and we recommend the severest penalty that you can render without mercy."

Immediately following the decision, screaming and crying filled the air. Never before in my entire life had I ever witnessed such a disturbance. The delegates began booing the decision. They began throwing every type of article into the air and the aisles. Some of those things were thrown toward the Jurors, fortunately no one was physically hurt. Yes, pandemonium had broken out, and the judge had an insurmountable task attempting to quiet and pacify that unruly crowd. He had completely lost control. Suddenly, a young Black American, one who had not lost faith in those things for which America stands, stepped forward, picked up a microphone, and began singing the "National Anthem." Only then was calm restored. My God, what a moment!

Judge Jim Crow then motioned for all of the members of the delegations to sit. He turned to the Black Americans and said, "Please remain standing until I have finished reading your sentence. As you know, it is not within my power to determine your guilt or your innocence, therefore, I have no choice but to abide by the law and pass judgment accordingly."

"I sentence you for life in a subservient position without ever obtaining freedom as long as you reside in the continental limits of the

'United' States of America. I further impose upon you the following restrictions:

1. You will, from this moment on, be called 'Negro' or 'Colored' or anything that 'White' persons choose to call you.

2. You will regard all 'White' persons as your masters, and you will give to them their due respect.

3. You will refer to all 'White' males as Mister and all 'White' females as Miss or Mrs.

4. You will be bought, traded, loaned and sold as property at the discretion and the convenience of all 'White' people.

5. You will teach your children that they should never think that they are equal to 'Whites'.

6. You will teach your children to be humble while in the presence of 'White' folk.

7. You women, both married and single, will never say 'no' to a 'White' man who chooses to lower himself to make love to you.

8. All children born to Black women and fathered by 'White' men will also be called 'Negro' or 'Colored.'

9. You will always ride the rear of public vehicles, and you will always give your seat to a 'White' person who may be standing.

10. You Black men will be faced with long prison terms or even death if you for once glance upon the body of a 'White' woman with lust in your eyes.

11. You will always do the menial tasks that 'White' persons choose not to do.

12. Whatever your accomplishments may be, they will not be included in the writing of American history.

13. Our Federal Bureau of Investigation will record and keep accurate records on all infamous acts committed by you whether you live in the North, the South, the East or the West.

14. You will be given the full penalty for all crimes committed by you against 'White' people, but another standard of justice will prevail when a 'White' person commits a crime against one of you.

15. You will never be allowed to marry a person of Caucasian descent.

16. You will never rebel against any 'White' person regardless as to what this individual might have done to you.

17. You will always wear balls and chains which will readily tell others of your lowly status in this life. When and if these balls and chains are every removed, your position on this earth will be determined by the color of your outer skin. Your skin color will be a constant reminder to future generations of 'White' Americans that you are not to be treated as equals.

18. According to our standards, you are the scum of our society and will always be known as America's Pariahs."

The judge kept reading, but my mind had begun to wander. I had heard too much already. When he finally finished reading that long list of punitive restrictions, he asked the Court Clerk to hand me a copy. As I reached out for it, I kept asking myself whether or not we had been given a fair trial. I could not understand why such a list had already been prepared. Did the judge really know in advance the verdict of the jury? I will always have my doubts about the validity of that "trial."

The judge immediately ordered four large deputies to bring in the balls and chains and to place them on my body as an example for the whole world to see. One was clamped to each leg and each arm. Each ball and chain weighed ten pounds, and the chains were long enough to drag on the ground.

When the chains were all in place, the judge asked me if I had anything else to say. I recall turning slowly toward my people, and I saw many of them crying openly. I saw many praying, and there were others who displayed expressions of uncontrollable grief. I think that it was these sights that told me that I must say something. I knew that I had not organized a speech, and even if I had, I do not think that it would have been appropriate at that time.

I knew that only the right words would soothe my people's battered feelings. What would I say? Where would I begin? I paused momentarily, knelt on one knee, and asked God Almighty to give me strength and to help me during that moment of crisis. Slowly I rose, faced the judge and said, "Yes, Your Honor, if it meets with your approval, I would like to say a few words."

I started toward the center of the platform and suddenly remembered the balls and chains which had been placed on the various parts of my body. Somehow, I managed to pull them with me. For a few seconds, the only sounds that were heard in that large arena were the sounds that came from those balls and chains.

When I reached the area just in front of the judge, I turned to my left, faced that huge gathering and began my recitation.

I said, "Your Honor, the Black Americans, for whom I speak, are deeply sorrowed for what has happened here today. Nevertheless, they are grateful to you for allowing me the opportunity to express for them their inner-most thoughts. I beg that you forgive me for my incoherent presentation as I humbly stand before you and this distinguished throng. But, how can one speak distinctly and with any degree of personal assurance after he and his people have been stripped of their dignity and their self respect as evidenced by the decision just rendered by this jury? How can one speak fluently after he and his people have just been told that they will be forever subjected to a life upon this earth in a capacity not fit for the lowest form of earthly creatures? How would any one react under similar circumstances?"

"The saddest thing about it all is the fact that it happened by a mere 12 votes. Never before had I known the importance of a single vote. Yes, just *one* vote would have made it possible for this 'trial' to have ended in a hung jury, and even that would have been of some relief."

"Your Honor, do allow me to start at the very beginning in order that everyone might know why we are here today. You see, it all began many years ago when the Portuguese started experimenting in the lucrative business called the Slave Trade. You Americans later tried your hand at this ancient past time, and it became an obsession with you. You traded insignificant articles to the African Chiefs for human lives. You broke up families. You caught, kidnapped, captured and chained my people against their will. You burned identifying marks on their bodies, and you fenced them as though they were animals. You stacked them in ships like sardines, and you transported them across the seas. You trained them to become your slaves who would answer to your every command. You caused my people to die of hunger, exposure and sickness simply because of your indifferent attitude toward their well being. Yet, you say that we are the ones who are uncivilized."

"You forced my people to discard their native tongue and to speak your language. You used every conceivable type of punishment to force your will upon my people. The most expendable thing to you was a life of a person of Negroid ancestry. You were unbearable, yet, you say that we are the heathens."

"When my people entered this country, you had not attempted to make them slaves, per se. The economic revolution in Europe, the elusiveness of the 'Whites,' the stubbornness of the Indians, and the ever—mounting workload here in America forced you to make that dreadful decision—a decision that you will be sorry for as long as America stands. You even kidnapped your own people from the streets and the jails in England and brought them to this land against their will, and you forced them to work for you. Yet, you say that we are the barbarians."

"You instituted punishments upon my people never before known to mankind. You cropped my people's ears. You cut off their fingers, arms and legs. You castrated our fathers and our brothers. You raped and impregnated our mothers and our sisters. You whipped my people unmercifully. You even killed my people, and yet, you say that we are the savages."

I then pointed an accusing finger at the jurors and said, "You have just rendered America's most distressing verdict. You have taken distorted truths and used them to satisfy your own desires. You had a choice to render a decision that would have resulted in either racial harmony or racial unrest, and you chose the latter. As a result of your decision, the future generations of all Caucasian Americans will suffer along with my people."

"Not one of you had a choice to be who you are today, and anyone of you could very well have been as Black as we are. Your verdict tells me that each of you is trying to play the role of God, and this was not meant to be. You, no doubt, think that your decision will bring 'White' folk pleasure, but to the contrary, it will only bring them more grief and more sorrow."

"You have made a mockery of the very things for which this country was founded. You know, as well as I, that in a Democracy—no man is any more or any less than another. You should be told that America will never really know the meaning of true democracy as long as this verdict is allowed to stand. My people and I wish for you to know also that your souls will never rest in peace, because of your decision on this very day."

"The most devastating facet of your decision was not so much the fact that you forced these penalties upon my contemporary brethren and me, but rather, you also imposed this harsh and unforgiving sentence upon future generations who have yet to be conceived. For this, you will never be exonerated."

"If only you could look into the future and witness the agony, the pain, the heartache, the guilt and the shame that all Americans will experience, I am reasonably certain that you would immediately reverse your decision."

I then looked directly at those delegates from North America and said, "As a result of this verdict, I shall make the following predictions:

1. I predict that this decision will give Caucasian Americans the 'green light' to disfigure and kill my people simply because they happen to be non-'White'.

2. I predict that my people will take these balls and chains, all forty pounds of them, and use them to strengthen their own bodies so that they, as individuals, will be stronger than any one of you.

3. I predict that, as a result of my people's body building philosophies, they will outstrip you in practically all physical endeavors whenever only ability counts.

4. I predict that one day you will do everything within your power to force my people to lose their identity by taking away their history, and they will demand that you also include their past in the American history texts.

5. I predict that one day one of you will 'free' my people, but as a result of this decision, his life will be shortened.

6. I predict that this country will one day be divided to the extent whereby only a situation short of a miracle will save it from eternal ruin.

7. I predict that the racial issue in America will become so intense until violence will become inevitable. You will fight a war, and the Northern region will defeat the Southern region.

8. I predict that the northern victors will attempt to reconstruct the southland. This attempt will fail miserably, and there will be a terrible recession. My people will again be the victims of oppressive and suppressive acts at the hands of evil Caucasian Americans.

9. I predict that, despite your many efforts to divide my people, they will one day become united as one and fight you in every way possible.

10. I predict that you will use bombs to destroy our churches, our homes, our automobiles and our children.

11. I predict that you will shoot and kill my people as they ride the highways of this nation, and the known killers will be set free to kill again.

12. I predict that you will one day talk of plans to destroy all of my people by poisoning them and by other devious ways.

13. I predict that you will attempt to send all of my people back to the continent of Africa, not realizing that America is as much their home as it is any Caucasian American who happens to call this country his or her home.

14. I predict that the federal government in this country will be strong when it comes to passing civil rights laws but weak when it comes to enforcing those very laws.

15. I predict that you will one day maintain a dual segregated school system in this country, and the Supreme Court will declare that system unconstitutional.

16. I predict that you will employ every deceitful means possible to avoid the integration of public schools.

17. I predict that some state 'Legislators' will close the schools to avoid school integration.

18. I predict that you will beat and fight our little children as they are left unprotected at school as one other manner by which to intimidate Black Americans and to keep the public schools segregated.

19. I predict that some of you will even attempt to take over the entire school system in your individual states to avert school integration.

20. I predict that you will not hear our cry for freedom until it becomes too late to help even yourselves.

21. I predict that your controlled news media will do much to keep the 'flames' of racial unrest burning so that harmony and calm cannot prevail.

22. I predict that you will bring unbearable pressures upon the lives of those Caucasian Americans who desire to aid their Black American brethren.

23. I predict that there will be Caucasian Americans who will fight along with my people in order to help them obtain those things which are rightfully theirs.

24. I predict that State and Federal legislatures will make attempts to deny elected Black American officials their Congressional seats primarily because of their race.

25. I predict that one day my people will converge upon this very city of Washington, D.C. by the thousands in a one-day vigil to denounce your heartbreaking decision.

26. I predict that the United States Supreme Court, despite its many discriminatory racial decisions over time, will stand up and lead the way toward freedom for *all* of America's citizens.

27. I predict that the Presidents of this great country will appoint known and proven racists to Federal judgeship positions after their terms in politics have ended.

28. I predict that you will do all within your power to keep my people subservient to you, but this will be to no avail.

29. I predict that you will restrict the liberties of your own Caucasian women in order to keep them from associating with men of other races.

30. I predict that your own women will one day come to realize that as long as my people are not free, she, too, will not be free.

31. I predict that the American Caucasian women will also find ways to repay you for all of the years that she has had to abide by your strict laws while you were able to love and impregnate women of all races.

32. I predict that the American Caucasian women, too, will one day be free to love and to marry anyone that they choose without regard to race, color or religion.

33. I predict that one day my people will become aware of the fact that you have exploited them and will demand equal justice and freedom as enjoyed by all other American citizens.

34. I predict that my people will begin a revolution in this country which will subside only after victory has been won.

35. I predict that my people will sacrifice some of their own lives, but they will burn down your cities in protest to this very decision.

36. I predict that many of you will preach integration of the races, but only a few of you will prove the sincerity of your words by practicing that which you preach.

37. I predict that there will be a day when my people will come from the rear of public vehicles and take their rightful places as drivers and operators of those very vehicles.

38. I predict that one day a heavyweight boxing champion of the world, or Negroid ancestry, will tell all concerned that there is nothing wrong with those persons who were not born of Caucasian descent.

39. I predict that you will force my people to join the armed services and fight to obtain and preserve freedom for others while my people themselves are still being denied their own freedom.

40. I predict that you will be repaid to the fullest for all of the sins that you have committed.

41. I predict that America will one day reveal to the whole world its ugliness, its hatred, its violence, its hostility, its oppression and its maliciousness when she begins to kill innocent women and children in Southeast Asia and other parts of the world.

42. I predict that my people will one day see you suffer as others have suffered as a result of your evil minds and deeds.

43. I predict that one of our offspring will one day travel this country preaching and teaching the philosophy of Black Power, and those two little words will shake the very roots of this nation.

44. I predict that the technique of non-violence to solve America's racial problems will be introduced by one of our distinguished brethren that will rattle the very conscience of this nation.

45. I predict that one of our own will rise to international fame and receive the greatest peace prize known to mankind for having done so very much to reverse this verdict.

46. I predict that one day Caucasian Americans will fall down on bended knees asking God for forgiveness for the many atrocities committed against my people, but my God will refuse to heed their plea.

47. I predict that my people will one day stand up proudly and say, 'Thank you God, for we are free at last.'"

I then stretched out both arms and spoke directly to those visiting delegates. I began by saying, "May I inform the thousands of you here, who are within the sound of my voice, that you have just witnessed a tragedy—a tragedy that will, no doubt, be considered as America's greatest mistake. I would be less than honest if I did not tell you that my people will, from this very moment, begin to smite the hand that wrote this verdict. My people will be willing to pay the supreme sacrifice to obtain those very things which God Almighty had intended for them. We are God's children, and because this is so, we cannot lose this battle."

Yes, it was at that very moment that I heard my people as they began to hum and sing. I looked around, and they were beginning to smile. I knew that I had said what they wanted to hear.

They began to clap their hands and pat their feet to the rhythm of a beautiful song—a song that I was hearing for the very first time. Listen! I can hear it now. (My people were humming the song "We Shall Overcome" and they had finally started singing it.) Just listen to the lyrics. Oh, how beautiful!

We shall overcome,
We shall overcome,
We shall overcome, some day.

Deep in my heart
I do believe
We shall overcome, some day!

My people continued to hum that song until I had ceased all talking. Yes, it was just as though it all happened yesterday. I can see my people now leaving that huge arena, two by two, arm in arm, just singing and humming that unforgettable song "We Shall Overcome."

My people then went into every community and into every village in this great country, and as a result of this verdict, they began serving their life sentence, without pardon, for "crimes" that they did not commit.

"Bring me solutions; I have enough problems."

Marion Barry
Ex-Mayor (Washington, D. C.)

SOLUTIONS TO AMERICA'S RACIAL PROBLEMS

It is my firm conviction that it will take all of us in this country (Black, White, Brown, Yellow and Red) to solve America's racial problems. Below are a few recommendations that I believe would serve as a great beginning:

Everyone should:

- Visit at least one of several museums that depicts African-American life.
- Take and/or retake a course in Civics and American History.
- Read at least three (3) books written by Black Historians or by Blacks who have experienced the brunt of raw discrimination in this country.

I suggest that you start this exercise by reading—

- *The Isis Papers* by Dr. Frances Crest Welsing,
- *From Slavery To Freedom* by Dr. John Hope Franklin and
- *The Mis-education of the Negro* by Dr. Carter G. Woodson.

If each citizen would do this, he or she would be better equipped to assist in tackling the problems of race in America. Furthermore, it would be much easier for the well-informed persons and groups to more-intelligently discuss and solve the many difficult and sensitive issues that face us all.

REPARATIONS

The word "Reparation" is defined as "compensation of money or materials (or both) payable to those injured as a result of another's actions and laws."

For crimes committed against the Jewish people, Germany officially apologized and chose reparations to rectify this horrible travesty that took place during World War II.

America selected the very same method when making amends with the Japanese-American people for having mistreated them (also during the Second World War).

In 1942, one year following the bombing of Pearl Harbor by Japan, America began uprooting Japanese-Americans from their homes and transferred them to World War II internment camps. More than 120,000 Japanese-Americans (70% of them U. S. Citizens) were transported by trains to ten camps scattered over six Western States and Arkansas. The Japanese-Americans were forced to stay in those camps until the war had ended.

However, after much debate in Congress, the American Government agreed to pay $1.25 billion to more than 60,000 survivors and their heirs.

During an emotional ceremony in the Great Hall of Justice, Attorney General Dick Thornborgh said, "By finally admitting a wrong, a nation does not destroy its integrity, but rather reinforces the sincerity of its commitment to the Constitution, and hence to its people. In forcing us to reexamine our History, you have made us only stronger and more proud."

Despite the fact that the leaders of this country chose to repay the Japanese-Americans before the African-Americans does not, in any way, lessen America's obligation to African-Americans and their heirs. Both groups were wronged, and both groups *will* be officially recognized and fully compensated for their pain.

America gave each Japanese-American survivor and his or her heirs an official apology plus a check in the amount of $20,000.00. It will be interesting for me to witness the "yardstick" that America chooses when trying to determine the correct compensation for each African-American survivor and their heirs for all of the atrocities committed against them. For example, what is a fair price to pay for working a man or a woman for a *lifetime* without either of them ever receiving *one* pay check?

This behavior, on the part of the ruling class in America, was so horrendous and so reprehensible until we, as a nation *today*, find it difficult to even hold discussions that would lead to a solution. Despite having said this, I am still convinced that America has always answered challenges when confronted and will once again refuse to disappoint and do the right thing. America will officially apologize and repay African-American Survivors and their heirs the full compensation that they are entitled.

Once this long-overdue act is finally complete, all of us can truly "EXHALE" and begin working together to help America regain its rightful place as the proven leader of the Free World!

INDIVIDUALIZED CONTRIBUTIONS

Several years ago, I asked Martin Luther King, III. this question: "Mr. King, in your opinion, what do you see as the solution(s) to African-American problems?" He said, "I don't have an answer to that question, but here is what I believe. Whatever it is that you and I have should be left at 'the table.' If each of us do this, I am convinced that one day someone will come along—look at all that we left—make sense of it and begin solving our many problems." I thanked him, and we went our separate ways.

Because I feel so passionate about those persons who removed obstacles and opened doors for those of us who followed, I have chosen to pay homage to them for the remainder of my days. This is one of those occasions.

I am leaving at "the table" two speeches that I wrote and delivered in the mid 1980s when I was a participant in Toastmasters. I entitled the speeches "Becoming Involved" and "The Portrait of an Artist" respectively. In each case, I highlighted some of those outstanding individuals who did so much to make our lives better.

Also, I am leaving at "the table" the name of one amazing woman—Hazel W. Mahone. Ms. Mahone's life was selected because of her rise from abject poverty to take her rightful place among America's great leaders in her chosen field—Education.

BECOMING INVOLVED

It was more than thirty years ago when my father said to me, "Son, the greatest joy that one can experience is knowing that he or she has done something to help somebody else."

I would like to share with you two such persons who have indeed earned my respect: one a woman, the other a man—one born into slavery, the other, four generations removed—one dead, one alive, both possessed an overwhelming desire to help other people.

Araminta Ross was the childhood name given to one of the world's most courageous women. I am talking about Harriet Tubman.

Harriet Tubman was born in 1821, or there about, in the state of Maryland. She was also born into slavery although she never thought of herself as a slave, but rather one to free the slaves. The history books tell us that Harriet Tubman, by way of the Underground Railroad, single-handedly freed more than 300 slaves in her lifetime. That is no small feat, ladies and gentlemen, for a young woman who had been denied all of her inalienable rights and one who fought one of the most bellicose systems of segregation known to man. Her friends and peers no longer called her Harriet; they called her Moses.

Yes, their Moses died in 1913, and on her tombstone were inscribed these words: "I never ran my train off the tracks, and I never lost a passenger." But, the quote that I remember best that was attributed to Harriet Tubman was the one when she said, "I have a right to liberty or death. If I can't have one, I will have the other." Such was the life of this remarkable woman and heroine we call Harriet Tubman.

Nevertheless, she left for generations to come a legacy of perseverance and courage. Randall Robinson was one who understood this legacy, for early on in his life he was taught the value and the virtue of courage and, if you will, stick-to-itiveness. Randall Robinson is the forty-three year old Richmond, Virginia born, Harvard University educated lawyer who heads the Free South Africa Movement in this country.

Randall Robinson understands that man's hatred of his own kind is both insane and unconscionable. Randall Robinson understands that racism is not confined to the shores of these United States. Randall Robinson understands that man's inhumanity to man is global in scope and widespread in practice. What Randall Robinson does *not* understand is why a country such as America—one that preaches freedom and majority rule the world over—chooses to align itself with a nation such as South Africa where racism is culturally enshrined, and minority rule—I said *minority rule*—is a way of life. That is perplexing to Randall Robinson.

When he visited South Africa more than eight years ago and saw first-hand how this vicious and repressive political regime treated its own majority, he knew then that he had to become involved. And, he did.

Yes, Harriet Tubman and Randall Robinson made decisions to help other people. As I look across this gathering today, I ask, "What about you?" Have you made a decision to help someone else lately? Do you feel that there is absolutely nothing left for you to do? I have some challenges for you. I dare you, any one of you, to spend the remainder of your days, if necessary, bringing the Indian people into the mainstream of American life. They have been excluded far too long already. I dare you to initiate programs that will educate all of America's illiterates. They, too, must share in the good life. I dare you to rewrite the American history books and include in them the contributions of all Americans. I am talking about Black, Brown, Red and Yellow Americans. The omissions and the distortions were much too maligned the first time around. But, my greatest challenge for you is—I dare you to dare to help somebody else today. Tomorrow is promised to none of us.

As I bring this brief talk to its end, with your permission, I would like to go back to the very beginning when I said to you what my father said to me many years ago, "Son, the greatest joy that one can experience is knowing the he or she has done something to help somebody else." If, in fact, my father's assessment is correct, then Harriet Tubman and Randall Robinson are undoubtedly two of the happiest people to have ever lived on planet earth.

Herman Melvin Witten, Sr.
April 1985

THE PORTRAIT OF AN ARTIST

I agree with the person who said, "The man who works with his hands is a laborer. The man who works with his hands and his head is a craftsman. But, the man who works with his hands, his head and his heart is an artist."

Today, I shall focus my attention on an artist of monumental proportions; an artist who has never painted a picture, an artist who has never sculptured a wad of clay, an artist who has never chiseled a piece of stone—yet—with the fifty states as his canvas, the multitude of races as his colors and a captivating voice as his brush, this artist transformed the conscience of a nation from a state of mistrust and discontent to one of faith and tolerance. And, he did it in only twelve short years. The Artist about whom I speak is none other than Dr. Martin Luther King, Jr.

My objective is three-fold. I will reconstruct for you Dr. King's entry into the civil rights arena. I will leave with you Dr. King's Legacy, and I will share with you a story about an important person whose life was affected because Dr. King had lived.

In order that I might accomplish this, I must first take you back in time to December 1, 1955, for it was on that Thursday afternoon in Montgomery, Alabama when Mrs. Rosa Parks (a Black seamstress) refused to give her seat on the bus to a man of European decent who was standing. Following her arrest, a bus boycott was planned. Dr. Martin Luther King, Jr. was chosen to lead. However, Dr. King was among the first to admit that if he is to lead, he would have to establish credibility, renew faith and instill confidence in the minds of his followers.

He then put together a meticulously-detailed and judiciously-orchestrated plan of action that was designed to bring to an end one of this city's more-shameful laws.

In his first speech that was given before the hastily—formed Montgomery Improvement Association he said, "One of the great glories of Democracy is the right to protest for right. If you protest courageously, yet with dignity and Christian love, when the history books are written in future generations, the Historians will have to pause and say, 'there lived a great people, a Black people, who injected new meaning and dignity into the veins of civilization.' This is our challenge and our overwhelming responsibility."

At that precise moment, Dr. Martin Luther King, Jr. declared war on America's number one social disease—racial inequality. One year and twelve days later, the Supreme Court ruled in favor of justice.

To prevent injustice for all time, Dr. Martin Luther King, Jr. left this four-part legacy:

- Be an emissary for justice; it is not *who* but *what* is right.
- Love and forgive your enemy as you wish to be loved and forgiven.
- Feed the hungry, clothe the naked and shelter the homeless.
- Do not spread the seeds of hate if you wish to harvest the fruits of love.

As I think about these codes of conduct, I am reminded of a short scenario that I will share with you. Last year, in the state of Alabama, a Black actress had just completed a stunning performance when she noticed a man crying. As this man approached her, he, too, offered his congratulations. And, almost as an afterthought he said, "Incidentally, I am the Judge who sentenced Dr. Martin Luther King, Jr. to jail, and I want you to know that I am sorry. I am very sorry." As they embraced, she whispered in his ear, "It's all right. *Everything* is all right." The Judge felt forgiven for the first time in seventeen years.

In closing, I wish to leave with you a few simple lines which, in my mind, best exemplify this great American Artist.

I know an artist who showed us the way-
    I know an artist who taught us fair-play-
His forgiving heart would put love to shame-
    Martin Luther King, Jr. was his name.

        Herman Melvin Witten, Sr.
        April 1986

"The greatest deterrent to racism is excellence."

Jesse L. Jackson

Hazel W. Mahone

HAZEL W. MAHONE

Ms. Hazel W. Mahone was born and reared in the state of West Virginia. After having finished Garnet High School in Charleston, she immediately enrolled as a Freshman at West Virginia State College. Four years later, Ms. Mahone had earned her Bachelor's Degree in the field of Education.

While waiting to be hired in her very first teaching assignment, she worked as an Assistant Playground Director. Soon thereafter, the Principal of Sissonville Elementary School (an all White School) contacted Ms. Mahone asking her to come in for an interview.

Ms. Mahone honored this request, and she found the Principal to be pleasant and engaging. He explained to Ms. Mahone that her credentials were exemplary and that he would love to have her come on staff. Despite his own favorable views on diversity, he explained to Ms. Mahone that there were deep-seeded negative attitudes that many Whites held toward Blacks and other minorities in that part of the state.

The Principal wanted Ms. Mahone to give serious thought before making such an important decision. Ms. Mahone wasted no time in responding. To this courageous Principal, she said, "I will accept this assignment, and I am prepared to begin immediately." The Principal was both surprised and pleased.

Ms. Mahone was elated to have been hired to her life-long "dream job." She assured the Principal that she would "make him proud." Their handshake sealed this deal, and both began preparing themselves for the fight of their professional lives.

The news of this hiring spread fast, and so did the animosity and the hatred of many of the community's White residents. From that very moment going forward, the Whites began harassing Ms. Mahone as she arrived in the morning and as she left the school building in the evening.

The Whites cursed her, called her horrible names and vowed that, "no 'N—r' will ever teach our children!" Ms. Mahone ignored all of the insults without saying one word. The Whites then organized a "sit-in" in Ms. Mahone's classroom every day for several months, but this remarkable teacher was not distracted.

Ms. Mahone's third grade students could not understand why their parents treated their "favorite teacher" so badly. After all, they loved her dearly and made their feelings known to all. This reciprocal love affair gave Ms. Mahone the courage and the capacity to continue doing what she was hired to do.

From the very first day, the local newspaper correspondents began to write a day-to day account of this story as events evolved. After all, this was the historical happening of that time and place.

After several months had passed, so had much of the anger and the hostility. Suddenly, the "sit-ins" discontinued and so did the negative language. The White parents started paying attention to their children's grade-point averages which were increasing exponentially. Finally, civility and reason had become the norm in the community making it possible for Ms. Mahone and her students to do many more things together.

One noteworthy thing that Ms. Mahone did occurred at the end of each working day. She would go to the home of *every* student who was absent due to illness and taught each child what he or she had missed that day. This practice was simply a part of her work day, and she never sought financial compensation, nor did she ever once complain.

It was this type of dedication and commitment that separated Ms. Mahone from all other teachers. Even those parents who fought her hiring reciprocated in kind by organizing a *"HAZEL W. MAHONE DAY"* honoring perhaps the greatest teacher to have ever taught at that school.

On that day, the accolades appeared endless. Each one, in its own way, said, "Please forgive our outrageous behavior. We honor you today for showing us the power of God's love" Also, they were saying "Thank you" to an ordinary woman who did ordinary things in an extra-ordinary way. Ms. Mahone graciously accepted all of their kind words and gifts and pledged to continue giving her best as long as she remained at Sissonville Elementary School.

Ms. Mahone taught two additional years there before submitting her resignation letter to the same Principal who placed his own job in jeopardy for hiring her. She thanked him profusely for believing in her and for taking the stand that he did without ever wavering. He also congratulated her for bringing diversity, humility and love to a once thankless and selfish school community. He said, "You, Ms. Mahone, set a standard that will not soon be matched, and you left a tradition that will *never* be forgotten. Furthermore, as earlier promised, you truly made me proud!"

Ms. Mahone, and her husband (Bill) moved to Battle Creek, Michigan. While there, her husband continued his work as a Supervisor in Job Corp, and she continued to juggle college and teaching.

Their next move was to the State of California. Ms. Mahone soon earned enough credits for two Masters Degrees before formally beginning a graduate program. Her doctoral studies had crowded in around her administrative position as head of a teacher intern program coordinated between the University of Pacific and the Sacramento City Schools. In 1975, Ms. Mahone received her Doctorate in Education Administration from California State University, Sacramento, California.

Dr. Mahone began her first collegiate assignment as an instructor at the University of Pacific, Stockton, California. While there, she taught the disadvantaged for two years, supervised Teacher Interns and served as the coordinator and Program Developer of Adult Education at Sacramento, City Unified School District.

She was selected to serve as the Assistant Superintendent, Adult Education Sacramento Unified School District. She was later elected to the Board of Directors of the 13,000 member association of California School Administrators. Dr. Mahone was second in command at the School

Board Association (a group whose members made policy for 90 percent of the children in the state). It was not surprising for those who knew her that she would also become the first Black to hold an administrative position in the California School Boards Association.

When the Superintendent's position became available in Dr. Mahone's hometown, as it was part of her responsibilities, she narrowed the candidates down to three and submitted their names to the local school board for their selection. Little did Dr. Mahone know, but the members of the board were so impressed with her input into this selection process, they chose not to accept any of the three candidates. Instead, they informed Dr. Mahone that they wanted her to personally fill this vacancy.

Dr. Mahone was pleasantly surprised yet cautiously optimistic because of the abruptness of this occurrence. After having carefully reviewed the entire offer, she recognized that this could be a "win-win" situation for the school system and for her. However, she was not willing to accept a $13,000.00 pay decrease in her yearly salary.

Dr. Mahone contacted the school board and informed them of her positive interest in their offer provided something be done about the salary discrepancy. She was told that they would begin right away working on the salary disparity and inform her of their decision.

The school board wasted no time before voting unanimously to increase the salary of the next Superintendent to satisfy Dr. Mahone's wishes. The Chairman of the local board said, "If we demand the best, we must be willing to pay for the best!"

When Dr. Mahone was notified of the school board's decision, she accepted the position and became the first Black and the first female to serve as Superintendent of Schools for the Sacramento City Unified School District, Sacramento, California.

Dr. Mahone's first day at work as Superintendent was on a Monday. Upon arriving at the office, she saw a large package on her desk. It contained a petition with several hundred signatures requesting that Dr. Mahone keep on staff the ever-so-popular "Dr. Clark" (not his real name).

Dr. Mahone said, "I knew that this incident had to be resolved *immediately*, or it could become a serious problem later." She began her own background check on "Dr. Clark" and scheduled an early meeting with him just two days later in her office.

When "Dr. Clark" arrived, Dr. Mahone welcomed him and said, "'Dr. Clark,' I saw the petition with all of the signatures that you left on my desk. That was quite impressive. My own inquiry of your tenure here revealed that you personally fought to obtain pay increases for the teachers and the administrators in this jurisdiction. I was also made aware that you had done many more positive things for persons on the Management side of this educational equation. But, 'Dr. Clark,' I did *not* see where you had done *anything* for the children! Please have your desk cleaned out by 5:o' clock PM on Friday of this week, because your replacement will be here at 8: o'clock Monday morning."

As "Dr. Clark" got up to leave, Dr. Mahone gave him his petition, wished him well and continued the process of notifying her own team who was then charged for educating all of the children in their region.

This decision set the tone for all others, and it demonstrated Dr. Hazel W. Mahone's Management style. This no-nonsense approach to solving problems has always been one of her strongest attributes.

For the next six years, while serving as the Superintendent of Schools, Dr. Mahone Set goals and exceeded most of them. She, once again demonstrated that becoming focused, being determined, staying persistent and displaying tenacity will always win out at the end of the day.

Dr. Mahone touched many lives from the time she first taught elementary school in Sissonville, West Virginia, Battle Creek, Michigan and Lewiston, California. She was also a member to the following organizations:

- Phi Delta Kappa Teachers Association as Dean of Pledges,
- Committeewoman of the Delta Sigma Theta Sorority,
- Vice President of Sacramento Area Black Educators and
- Continuing Education Association.

Some of Dr. Mahone's community service activities included:

- The Board of Directors of United Way,
- Sacramento Urban League,
- NAACP Creative Career,
- YMCA,
- Planned Parenthood,
- California State University—Fine Arts,
- Visiting Nurses Association,
- Sacramento's Alumni Association and
- Community Service Planning Council.

Dr. Mahone's awards over the years were numerous. Here is a list of only a few of them:

- The Sacramento Area Black Educator of the Year Award,
- The Omega Psi Phi Community Service Award,
- NAACP Woman of the Year Community Service Award,
- Red Cross Service Award (2 each)
- National Council of Adult Educators Award for Outstanding Statewide Service,
- The Association of California School Administrators President's Award, and
- The American Association of School Administrators Award (Affiliated with the Ford Foundation).

At the time of this writing, Dr. Mahone was well into her "third career" (her words). She had just completed six years as a teacher at California State University in Sacramento, California.

On January 23, 2008, Dr. Mahone received her tenure and a promotion to Professor. Those two feats thrilled her immensely.

In my last interview with Dr. Mahone, I asked her to tell me what made her most-proud among all of her many accomplishments? Without hesitation, she said, "During my professional life, I prepared students to become teachers; teachers to become principals and, principals to become superintendents. And, I truly loved that more than anything else in the world."

I personally thanked her for all of the time that she had extended to me for the interviews, and I reminded her that the thousands of students that she taught during her long and illustrious career will not soon forget the name—Dr. Hazel Witten Mahone.